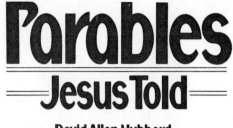

Parables
Jesus Told

David Allan Hubbard

Pictures
of the
New Kingdom

InterVarsity Press
Downers Grove
Illinois 60515

InterVarsity Press is the book-publishing division of Inter-Varsity Christian
Fellowship, a student movement active on campus at hundreds of universities,
colleges and schools of nursing. For information about local and
regional activities, write IVCF, 233 Langdon St., Madison, WI 53703.

Distributed in Canada through InterVarsity Press, 1875 Leslie St., Unit 10,
Don Mills, Ontario M3B 2M5, Canada.

ISBN 0-87784-471-2

Printed in the United States of America

Library of Congress Cataloging in Publication Data

Hubbard, David Allan.
    Parables Jesus told.

    1. Jesus Christ–Parables–Sermons.   2. Baptists–
Sermons.   3. Sermons, American.   I. Title.
BT375.2.H75   226'.806   81-8211
ISBN 0-87784-471-2   AACR2

15	14	13	12	11	10	9	8	7	6	5	4	3	2	1
93	92	91	90	89	88	87	86	85	84	83	82	81		

Preface   7

Conclusion   93

Preface

Parables form the core of Jesus' teaching. Approximately one-third of all the sayings credited to him in the synoptic Gospels are parabolic in form. These realistic stories, based on events from everyday life, grounded their divine truth in the soil of human history and experience. The sublime message of the Master was tethered to the world of farm and marketplace, and not allowed to float aimlessly into an atmosphere of abstract speculation. In Jesus, God's eternal Word had become flesh. In the parables, that Incarnation was reinforced by literary power and grace.

Understanding the parables, then, leads us to the center of what Jesus was saying and doing. These illustrative stories tell us how God is working in human circumstances, what our response to that work should be—with repentance a dominant theme

—and, especially, who God is. In stories, Jesus interpreted his own mission, which had at its heart his
purpose of showing us the glory, power and love of
God the Father. This picture of God dominates the
parables; they can be called theology pure and proper.
The lead figure in the stories was inevitably the God
of heaven. Whether in the guise of farmer sowing
seed, judge settling accounts, master paying wages or
entrusting talents, father arranging a wedding or welcoming a prodigal, or shepherd searching for strays,
the person behind the simile is always the LORD
Almighty to whom Jesus taught us to pray, "our
Father."

The purpose of this book is simply to communicate
the meaning of each story so that the compelling truth
of God's kingship will clutch us in its claims and
commandeer us to be responsible citizens of that
kingdom. The method used is equally simple: (1) we
look at the *setting* of each story in the life of Jesus to
understand the context which gave rise to it; (2) we
sketch the main *message*, assuming that parables aim
to teach one major point, trying to hear precisely what
Jesus was teaching and (3) we state the *demand* that
each lesson carries, knowing that any word or deed of
Jesus called for personal obedience as well as for intel-
lectual assent.

If this approach seems so methodical as to border
on monotony, it may still be a welcome relief from the
casual ad-libbing from which the parables have so
often suffered in our frenzied attempts to make them
relevant. Discipline in the way we try to discern the
truths of Scripture is as essential for Christians as
dedication to the truths we discover.

These chapters appeared first as messages on "The

Joyful Sound" radio broadcast. Their written form owes much to the labors of my wife, Ruth, who also typed the manuscripts. I see almost daily in her life pictures of the joy, the power and the obedience of the new kingdom.

1

The Sower and the Seed

The Impact of the King's Word

Matthew 13:1-9, 18-23

AS A STORYTELLER JESUS has no peer. The set of stories with which he captivated his first hearers have lost none of their appeal. Their power, their clarity, their earthiness, their simplicity have seized the attention of hearers in every century, every climate, every culture.

Every bar or pub knows clever storytellers whose wit and humor serve as life rafts for men and women drowning in a sea of boredom. But Jesus was no entertainer. He did not regale his followers with amusing stories designed to help them wile away their lonely evening hours. His mission was not to amuse but to convict. He came for higher purposes than to ease the anguish of jaded spirits with stories of traveling salesmen or shaggy dogs.

Every generation has had its sages who, with barbed tongue or wry smile, have unmasked or disarmed the elite. But Jesus was no political pundit. He did not devote his powers of observation and description to lampooning the antics of Caesar or the comical attempts of Herod to ape the emperor. His mission was not to expose the foibles of the political system but to call men and women to repentance. He did not come to satirize the political scene like the Roman writer Juvenal or to caricature it like the Oklahoman humorist Will Rogers. Redemption, not correction, was his aim.

The world has long profited from wise teachers who have shrewdly observed the benefits and pitfalls of certain patterns of behavior and communicated these observations in sayings deftly shaped to hook into our memories. But Jesus was no moralist. He did not exhort his students to do better or to try harder. His mission was not to reform but to renew. Jesus came to do what neither the proverbs of Solomon nor the sayings of Benjamin Franklin were meant to do. His purpose was not just to improve our conduct but to re-create our lives.

Jesus was a master storyteller. He was no humorist, though his stories are touched with humor. He was no political commentator, though his stories are fraught with significance for the structures of society. He was no moralist, though his stories have had a transforming impact on human behavior. For the secret of the power of Jesus' stories, we must look beyond techniques of communication and insights into human nature. It is the subject matter of the stories that accounts for their popularity and their effectiveness.

The Theme of Themes

Jesus' parables, as we call these stories, focus on one magnificent theme—the kingdom of God. This is not surprising when we remember that the chief purpose of Jesus' coming was to establish this kingdom. John the Baptist, sent by God to prepare Jesus' path, had one basic message: "Repent, for the kingdom of heaven is at hand" (Mt 3:1). And when Jesus himself came into public prominence, it was reported that "he went about all Galilee, teaching in their synagogues and preaching the gospel of the kingdom and healing every disease and every infirmity among the people" (Mt 4:23). The gospel was the good news that God, here and now, was establishing his rule among men and women. Jesus' miracles demonstrated this royal rule that neither illness, demons nor death could successfully oppose.

This theme—the kingdom of God—was not new to Jesus' countrymen, especially those learned in the Scriptures. They knew that God wanted to be ruler of his people. They knew that he had established his lordship over them at the exodus under Moses and had confirmed his lordship during the days of the monarchy under David and Solomon. They also believed that the time would come when God would again make his glory known among them through David's great son. But in the meantime that kingly glory, that majestic reign was an experience known only in heaven, celebrated only by the angels.

Now John had come preaching that it was approaching—the kingdom was about to come. And Jesus had come preaching that it was here—the kingdom revealed in his love, his wisdom and his power.

The response to John and to Jesus was conflict. Many Jewish leaders longed for the kingdom to come. None expected the kingdom to come in this way. A gruff desert prophet? An itinerant Galilean carpenter? How could they be the stuff of which the kingdom of God was made?

It was to answer questions like those that Jesus began to teach in parables. If his miracles demonstrated the power of the kingdom and the compassion of the King, then his parables explained the kingdom, spelling out its purpose, nature and timing.

The parables, then, are not stories that illustrate timeless religious truths. They are lessons that Jesus taught his disciples in specific contexts to help them understand the kingdom. The first thing we need to know, then, is the *setting* of a parable. What gave rise to it? What questions were Jesus' friends asking that the parable was designed to answer?

Next, we try to grasp the *message*. Ordinarily a parable has one main point. It is not teaching a whole curriculum; it is getting at one need. The details and the movement of the story are designed to lead the hearer to an understanding of that one point—the truth carried by the parable.

Finally, we look for the *demand* that the parable's message lays on us. Parables were given not only for understanding but also for obedience, which is the best test of understanding. Only when we act on what a parable has taught have we really caught its truth.

The Setting: Conflict and Doubt

Jesus began to use parables at a crisis point in his ministry. His mighty miracles and bold claims had put him in conflict with the Jewish leaders, especially the Pharisees who saw themselves as guardians of the traditions and protectors of Israel's true faith. The conflict widened when Jesus violated the sabbath laws by plucking grain (Mt 12:1-8) and healing a man with a withered hand while in the synagogue (12:9-14). At that point Matthew notes, "But the Pharisees went out and took counsel against him, how to destroy him" (12:14).

The gap grew wider still when Jesus healed a man made blind and dumb by demonic power. "It is only by Beelzebul, the prince of demons, that this man casts out demons," was the Pharisees' rash verdict (12:24). The Master's response was equally harsh: "You brood of vipers! how can you speak good, when you are evil?" (12:34).

A conflict this sharp could not help but raise doubts in the minds of that straggling band of believers who had left everything to follow him. True, he had told them that they would be sent "out as sheep in the midst of wolves" (10:16). But they had just begun to realize how fiendish the wolves were and how vulnerable the sheep! What about the kingdom, was it really here? Why did the people who should have known most about it and should have most warmly welcomed it now pit themselves against it?

The Message: Bad Soils and Good

The story that Jesus told sketched a scene every one of his hearers had watched many times. A farmer would walk across his small patch of land clad in his loincloth with a bag of seed cinched about his waist. With each stride his hand clutched a scoop of seed and tossed it beside him to the ground. Four different things might happen to the seed. Jesus' hearers knew them well; they were no strangers to the hazards of farming.

Since there were few fences or hedges to divide plot from plot, paths were sometimes used to mark boundary lines. Furthermore, the farmer's own steps would pound a path on which some seed was bound to fall. Frequently, Jewish farmers would first sow their lands and then plow to turn the soil and cover the seed. Some of the seed was lost on the packed-down dirt and became ready prey for the ever-present birds (13:4).

In other places stones lay just below the surface. The seed that fell there would spring up rapidly, warmed by the heat that the stones retained. The rocky terrain of Judah and Galilee has frustrated generations of farmers from the days of Gideon to the modern *kibbutzim*. On such shallow soil, plants grow quickly and die quickly, robbed of roots and victimized by the desert sun (13:5).

Still other seed was choked out by the thorn bushes, weeds of unbelievable vitality. The farmer had probably chopped them down or burned them, but their roots remained ready to nourish their evil growth and menace the life of the good seed (13:7).

But the fourth type of soil was good—not packed hard, not deceptively shallow, not infiltrated by the seeds and roots of thorn bushes. It was soil that gave the seed the room and the nurture it needed to do its dying and multiplying in that miracle we call growth (13:8).

Jesus put the spotlight on the *soils* because, as in farming, the seed is assumed to be good. Here we know the seed is good because Jesus interpreted it as "the word of the kingdom." What is sown is the news that the kingdom is here and people must repent and receive it. Jesus and his disciples had been broadcasting that message throughout the land. But just as some seed does not grow because it falls on soil unsuited for its growth, so the announcement of the kingdom is received in different ways by different persons.

Some, like beaten soil, will have closed minds. They would not receive the kingdom if God himself handed it to them. Satan, like the greedy birds, snatches the word from their minds (13:19).

Others seem to grasp the message and to rejoice in the news that God is making known his reign among the human family, but they have no staying power. Opposition from friends and family, and persecution from their enemies cause them to draw back. At first glimpse they appear to be sons and daughters of the kingdom. But they have no roots and their full allegiance lies elsewhere (13:20-21).

Still others hear the good news but cannot fight the distraction of worldliness, especially the desire for things. Like thorns, these appetites stifle the hunger and thirst for God's righteousness which characterize true citizens of the kingdom.

The Demand: Openness and Trust

Yes, says Jesus to his followers, you can expect many people not to listen. What is good news to you—that God is moving among you in a fresh way—is not good news to others. But that does not mean that the news is not good. And that does not mean that many will not receive it and let it thrive within them. Indeed, one hundredfold, sixtyfold and thirtyfold are the factors by which the God of all growth, the Lord of all harvest, will multiply his seed.

We, like this parable's first hearers, are to *be open* like good soil to the word of the kingdom; we are to *trust* the God who cares for both seed and soil to work his magnificent growth.

Jesus' parable leaves us with only one question. Not a question about his power and glory—those he has made plain. He questions our receptiveness: what kind of soil are we?

Prayer: Lord of the seed and the harvest, plant your truth deep within my life that it may resist the lure of wealth, the tug of distraction and the greed of Satan. Let it grow at your pace and by your grace that I may be a true child of your kingdom, bent on doing your will. Through Jesus Christ I pray. Amen.

2

The Wheat and the Weeds

The King's Judgment

Matthew 13:24-30, 36-43

THE CONTRAST WAS STARTLING. The crowds were perplexed, and so were Jesus' disciples. What they expected and what they saw were two different things. They heard the language, but it did not fit their definitions.

They puzzled over the picture of God's kingdom seen in the book of Daniel and the picture that Jesus presented. The vocabulary was the same—the kingdom of God or kingdom of heaven—but the meaning seemed different.

Their perplexity was understandable. They were well acquainted with Nebuchadnezzar's vision, as described by Daniel:

You saw, O king, and behold, a great image. . . . The head of this image was of fine gold, its breast and arms of silver, its belly and thighs of bronze, its legs of iron, its feet partly of iron and partly of clay. As you looked, a stone was cut out by no human hand, and it smote the image on its feet of iron and clay, and broke them in pieces; then the iron, the clay, the bronze, the silver, and the gold, all together were broken in pieces, and became like the chaff of the summer threshing floors; and the wind carried them away, so that not a trace of them could be found. But the stone that struck the image became a great mountain and filled the whole earth. (Dan 2:31-35)

They were also well acquainted with Daniel's interpretation of the dream in which the metals of the image were said to represent a series of kingdoms, each less splendid than the previous. Firmly fixed in their minds was the meaning of the stone that shattered the image:

And in the days of those kings the God of heaven will set up a kingdom which shall never be destroyed, nor shall its sovereignty be left to another people. It shall break in pieces all these kingdoms and bring them to an end, and it shall stand for ever. (Dan 2:44)

But on to the scene came a desert prophet, cloaked in camel's hair, and a carpenter from an obscure village of Galilee. Together the prophet and the carpenter could not field a platoon, let alone an army. This talk of a kingdom was well and good. But where was the proof that Daniel's God was on the move?

The Setting: Kingdom but Not Glory

The disciples must have doubted whether they had cast their lot with one who could lead them to victory. Would God's righteousness really win in a world that seemed so set against it? Granted that the kingdoms of the world needed crushing, was their Master powerful enough to bring that judgment? And if he were, why had he not already done so?

The disciples had every right to believe that God's kingdom and God's judgment would go hand in hand. John the Baptist had said as much at the beginning of Jesus' ministry when he warned the Pharisees and the Sadducees, "Even now the axe is laid to the root of the trees; every tree therefore that does not bear good fruit is cut down and thrown into the fire" (Mt 3:10). Jesus himself, as John described him, was to play the key role in this judgment: "His winnowing fork is in his hand, and he will clear his threshing floor and gather his wheat into the granary, but the chaff he will burn with unquenchable fire" (3:12).

Bold pronouncements—but what had happened since? John had been slapped into prison. And Jesus, far from winnowing the wheat from the chaff, was eating with tax collectors and sinners. Yet he sensed their concern and responded with the parable of the wheat and the weeds. It was his basic answer to the question, how can there be a kingdom without glory, especially a kingdom without the glory of judgment?

The Message: Judgment... but Not Yet

Jesus knew that the impatience of his friends had

been experienced by some of Israel's noblest souls in bygone days. Habakkuk, for instance, had begged God to show his glory by judging the sins of Judah, sins that God had commanded Habakkuk to denounce:

> O LORD, how long shall I cry for help,
>> and thou wilt not hear?
> Or cry to thee "Violence!"
>> and thou wilt not save? . . .
> So the law is slacked
>> and justice never goes forth. (Hab 1:2, 4)

At about the same time, Jeremiah poured out his vexation to God in words that rang with impatience:

> Why does the way of the wicked prosper?
>> Why do all who are treacherous thrive? . . .
> Pull them out like sheep for the slaughter,
>> and set them apart for the day of slaughter.
> (Jer 12:1, 3)

What kind of king is it that allows unrighteousness to go unpunished? And how can any program claim to be God's kingdom, when sin is yet rampant? If Habakkuk and Jeremiah could raise such questions, how much more could the followers of a Teacher who claimed that in him the kingdom had come?

Carefully and clearly, the master Teacher set out to put these problems to rest. He used a story to do so—both because he wanted to baffle the general public who were not prepared to accept his royal claims and because he wanted to lodge his words deep in the memories of his loved ones so that they could ponder them and pass them on to others.

The parable is found in Matthew 13:24-30. A man sowed good seed in his field only to find that bad seed was also growing in it, sown at night by his enemy. The man's servants were eager to root out the weeds, but the owner forbade them, fearing that good wheat would be lost in the process. "Wait until harvest," he ordered. "Then the reapers will be able to tell weeds from wheat and will burn the weeds and store the wheat."

The weeds, or tares as they are sometimes called, were probably *darnel*, a poisonous grass that in its early growth looks like wheat and is about the same height. When wheat is ready for harvest, however, it can be easily distinguished from darnel by its color and the shape of the heads of grain. Since all harvesting was done by hand instruments—knives, sickles and scythes—the harvesters would have little problem telling which was which.

We must judge the meaning of the story from Jesus' interpretation of the details: the *sower* of the good seed is Jesus himself, the Son of man. The *field* is the world, while the *good seed* stands for the sons of the kingdom and the *bad seed* for the sons of Satan, sown by the devil. The *harvest* is the close of the age when the angels will be the reapers (13:36-43).

The kingdom of God (Matthew calls it the kingdom of heaven in keeping with Jewish custom) does not put an *immediate* end to the evils of this age. Good and evil, those who are loyal to God and those who follow Satan, will live side by side in society until the end of the age. This mixture is part of the mystery of God's kingdom.

To put it another way, Jesus is telling us that God's kingdom is both present and future. It is already here, yet it is still coming. It is here in the love and power which Jesus demonstrated; it is still to come in its judging glory. It is here in its life-changing might;

it is not yet here in its world-shaking majesty.

The Demand: Patience but Not Complacency

The story of the wheat and weeds insists that we be patient but not complacent. It tells us to wait but not to loiter.

The *importance* of our patience shows in the fact that we are the harvest, not the harvesters. How we long to take the sickle in hand and wade into the weeds of unbelief and unrighteousness that grow chest-high around us! We yearn for judgment to come, for God to clear away all that clutters his field and threatens to poison his people. But that is God's task, not ours. He will do it by his schedule, not by ours.

The *reasons* for our patience are plain. First, the lordly triumphant Son of man is in charge of the whole process. He it was who sowed the seed; he it will be who sends the harvesting angels. The outcome is not in doubt. Patience does not mean uncertainty.

But what about the devil and his poisonous seeds? Is there not the possibility that they will crowd out the wheat? "Not so," says Jesus. His whole life proved him right, for he deliberately and consistently cast out demons to show his power over Satan's realm. Christ had bound the devil as one binds a strong man, and now he was plundering Satan's house (Mt 12:28-29).

Second, we can be patient because we will share in that victory: "Then the righteous will shine like the sun in the kingdom of their Father" (13:43). Mixture we can bear; injustice we can put up with; our struggles with the children of that other kingdom we can endure. Today's sufferings are paltry when compared with the future glory that God has reserved for his own.

Prayer: Father, help us to wait in patience for the climax of your program. Let us not wait with faces darkened by uncertainty. But let the assurance of that future glory start us shining now as our lives are lit by your love and grace. Through Christ, the conquering Son of man. Amen.

3

The Seed That Grows Silently

The Presence of the King's Influence

Matthew 13:31-33; Mark 4:26-29

THERE WERE NONE OF THE trappings of royalty. The scenes were hardly courtly. Debates in the market-places, sermons in the synagogues, lessons on the quiet hillsides—these were the curriculum of a teaching prophet, not the protocol of a king.

To be sure, there were miracles. The sick were healed; the blind were given sight; the lame were sent away running; those possessed by demon power were given a new freedom. But these were deeds of a wonder worker, another Moses or a second Elijah, not the actions of one claiming to be a king.

Still, there was constant talk of kingship. It was the theme of Jesus' preaching; it was the message he sent his men to proclaim. Not the talk of a *future* kingdom which the prophets had predicted and for which Israel's faithful were yearning, but of a *present* kingdom, a divine rulership demonstrated then and there. Jesus and his followers announced, "The kingdom of heaven is at hand" (Mt 10:7).

Yet there was *no general recognition of Jesus' authority*. Whatever else a kingdom must have, it cannot function unless its authority is recognized—talk of a kingdom seems just talk. The chief spokesman of this kingdom was a mere carpenter who, far from behaving like royalty, marked himself as a lawbreaker by working on the holy day of rest.

When the Pharisees rebuked him for this unlawful conduct, he added to their outrage by linking himself with good King David. He reminded his chiders that Israel's great monarch had himself violated the law by eating bread that was forbidden to anyone but a priest (Mt 12:1-8).

The indignation caused by this comparison was further inflamed by a question the common people began to ask: "Can this be the Son of David?" (12:23). What gave rise to the question—which might be paraphrased "Is Jesus really the Messiah?"—was the miraculous healing of a blind, speechless demoniac. Though the ordinary citizenry interpreted the healing as possible evidence that the Messiah had come, the Pharisees had a contrary explanation: "It is only by Beelzebul, the prince of demons, that this man casts out demons" (12:24).

There was also *no display of worldly majesty*. The

Master possessed no palace on the lofty heights of Mount Zion. He once remarked that he had no place to lay his head. He mounted no throne, wielded no scepter, wore no crown. Talk of his kingdom caused no rumbling in Caesarea, Rome's eastern capital, let alone on the banks of the Tiber where Caesar was occupied with what the world deemed far more important matters. A tattered band of fishermen and peasants, even with a tax collector thrown in, was hardly the stuff of which revolutions were shaped or kingdoms were built. Even David had a band of seasoned soldiers at his side when he succeeded Saul as king.

There was *no emphasis on a family dynasty*. Not only was Jesus unmarried, a virtually unforgivable state for one who wanted to perpetuate a kingdom, but his attitude toward his own family was puzzling. Once, when someone interrupted his teaching to tell him that his mother and brothers were standing outside, he responded to the man with a gentle rebuff: "Who is my mother, and who are my brothers?" Then, gesturing toward his disciples, Jesus answered his own questions: "Here are my mother and my brothers! For whoever does the will of my Father in heaven is my brother, and sister, and mother" (Mt 12:48-50).

Jesus' disciples must have been as puzzled as the rest of his hearers. They treasured the intimacy of their friendship with the Master. But were they really kin to royalty? Were they fit to be princes in the kingdom? They were not from the right clan or family. They were not descendants of David, whose kingdom the prophets like Isaiah, Micah and Jeremiah had proclaimed.

The Setting: Anxiety over Small Beginnings

Jesus told three stories—the parable of the mustard seed, the parable of the leaven and the parable of the seed that grows silently—to ease the disciples' anxiety (Mt 13:31-33; Mk 4:26-29). They had been taught that the kingdom of God would come with volcano-like force. But, at that point, Jesus' ministry seemed more like a quiet campfire. *Is the kingdom really here?* was the disciples' question. They did not doubt that the kingdom would come, but they were unsure that it had already arrived.

The Savior seized upon their question to help them understand the mysteries of God's kingdom. *Mystery*, as the New Testament uses the term, means a truth previously unknown to God's people but now made clear. The simplest definition of *mystery*, therefore, is "newly revealed truth."

The story of the tiny mustard seed (which, in Galilee, grows into a shrub eight to ten feet tall) and the story of the leavened dough (which is hidden in a huge tub of meal and permeates all of it) are designed to reveal a new truth about the kingdom and to confirm the kingdom's arrival.

The story of the seed that grows while the farmer sleeps speaks to a further, yet related, question: *Do we have the resources to bring about the kingdom?* For at least Simon the Zealot and Judas Iscariot this seemed a very natural question. They had once been adherents of a party in Palestine known as the Zealots, sworn enemies of the pagan power of Rome. In fact during Jesus' boyhood the party had fomented a short-lived revolt against the Romans but did not have the resources to set up a new kingdom.

The Message: Encouragement by God's Sovereignty

Jesus' answers to these questions are direct, though the story form keeps them from being painfully blunt: Yes, surprisingly the kingdom *is* present, as a tiny seed contains the whole potential of a mustard shrub. Yes, the kingdom is present, though in hidden form, as a lump of leavened dough would be hidden in a mass of meal. But no, the kingdom does not depend on human resources—it is like a seed which grows without human care until the harvest. Be encouraged by God's sovereignty, for from seedlike small beginnings a large bush will grow. From a hidden lump a whole tub of flour will be leavened. The kingdom will grow through God's power, not through human ingenuity.

The message of God's surprising sovereignty is reinforced by the images of the tree and the leaven. Jesus' description of the tree in whose branches the birds find nest would have reminded his followers of Nebuchadnezzar's vision in the days of the prophet Daniel: "I saw, and behold, a tree in the midst of the earth; and its height was great.... The beasts of the field found shade under it, and the birds of the air dwelt in its branches." Daniel interpreted, "The tree you saw, which grew and became strong... —it is you, O king.... Your greatness has grown and reaches to heaven, and your dominion to the ends of the earth" (Dan 4:10, 12, 20, 22).

The true tree, Jesus says, is not Nebuchadnezzar's kingdom, which was stripped and then chopped down in the vision (4:13-16), but God's kingdom, present now in seed form. The Lord of surprises has taken an illustration of what was originally a flourishing pagan empire and has used it to tell us to whom the universal kingdom really belongs.

From the days of their first Passover in Egypt, the people of Israel viewed leaven as a symbol of impurity. At the annual feast of unleavened bread they were forbidden to eat it for seven days (Ex 12:18-20). Similarly, the bread that the priests ate beside the altar was to be unleavened (Lev 10:12). Jesus himself sometimes used leaven as a sign of contamination: "Take heed and beware of the leaven of the Pharisees and Sadducees" (Mt 16:6).

The true leaven, Jesus said, the good leaven whose hidden influence will ultimately penetrate all of life, is not the corruption of pagan philosophy nor the contagion of the Pharisees' legalism. It is the power and glory of God's sovereignty, which will challenge and drive out all other claims to rulership.

The Demand: Anticipation of God's Victory

Parables are never given just for information. They demand our response. Jesus' aim was not just to sharpen the thinking of his disciples. It was to shape their living.

Don't be discouraged by small beginnings. Don't be disheartened because God's work seems hidden. Don't be depressed by your inadequate human resources. All that is needed for God's ultimate victory is already at work.

If an itinerant teacher and his motley band scarcely look like a royal entourage, remember the mustard seed. Then trust God and wait. If the craftsman from Nazareth seems to be constantly discounted and even brutally rebuffed, if his influence seems hardly to ripple the waters of Roman rule, remember the leaven. Then trust God and wait. If the entire resources of Jesus and his followers seem inadequate to start a small business, let alone establish a worldwide kingdom, remember the seed that grows while the farmer sleeps. Then trust God and wait.

Even after nineteen centuries, during which that mustard seed has taken root and thrust out branches, we wonder whether God is truly in control. Even after nearly two millennia of Christian leavening, the lump of life still seems godless. Even after God's people have expanded to a global multitude counted in the scores of millions, our resources seem inadequate to the task.

Most of what went with royalty was absent from Jesus' ministry. And the situation is no different with us. Our churches are small and struggling; our enterprises lack prestige and influence. In wealth, in numbers, in reputation we live in the shadow of great universities, giant laboratories, massive industries and mammoth governments.

But it is we—not they—who live in anticipation of victory. God's kingdom is here now and yet to come. On that we can depend, and we do and will share in it. Our God is the God of the tiny mustard seed, the hidden leaven and the silent growth. His are the kingdom, the power and the glory. And we belong to him.

Prayer: Lord of secret growth, Lord of hidden power, teach us to trust your timing, to believe in your presence and to wait for your victory. Through Jesus Christ who makes this possible, we pray. Amen.

4

The Good Samaritan

A New Style of Royalty

Luke 10:25-37

THE DISCIPLES WERE ELATED at their newfound power. The lawyer was puzzled by the bold claims of Jesus. The stage was set for one of the most memorable moments in Jesus' ministry.

Jesus had sent his disciples out two by two to the villages and towns of Judea and Galilee with the instructions, "Whenever you enter a town and they receive you, eat what is set before you; heal the sick in it and say to them, 'The kingdom of God has come near to you' " (Lk 10:8-9). But the kingdom of God meant not only healing to those who received its message but also judgment to those who did not: "But whenever you enter a town and they do not receive you, go into its streets and say, 'Even the dust of your town that clings to our feet, we wipe off against you; nevertheless know this, that the kingdom of God has come near.' I tell you, it shall be more tolerable on that day for Sodom than for that town" (vv. 10-12).

With this commission Jesus' disciples went out with boldness and returned with joy: "Lord, even the demons are subject to us in your name!" (v. 17). They had seen the King's power at work firsthand, and they were elated.

The lawyer, on the other hand, was puzzled. A devout and learned teacher of Jewish law, he had wondered how a peasant from Nazareth could claim to be the representative of God's kingdom. He was also baffled about Jesus' attitude toward the law. How could God's emissary take such liberties with the sacred sabbath? What did this wandering prophet, this itinerant teacher, really believe?

The Setting: A Question about Ultimates

As usual, Jesus was not declaring a vague spiritual principle when he told the good Samaritan's story; he was responding to a specific question sparked by his ministry. The lawyer's motive for asking it was neither idle curiosity nor deep spiritual hunger. It was something in between, something that Luke described as putting Jesus "to the test." The question was a good one, even if the motive behind it was not: "Teacher, what shall I do to inherit eternal life?" (v. 25).

The lawyer was trying to probe Jesus' attitude

toward the Jewish law, his own field of expertise and the point at which Jesus seemed most vulnerable. The lawyer seemed to have the Old Testament on his side. After all, didn't Moses say (Lev 18:5) that life comes by the keeping of the law?

As the master Teacher, Jesus knew both where the questioner was leading and how best to help him learn, so he tossed the question right back to him without elaboration: "What is written in the law? How do you read?" In focusing on the Old Testament law, Jesus refused to make the lawyer his adversary. Instead he joined him in *acknowledging the authority of the Scriptures*. The lawyer had asked a spiritual question, a spiritual question on an ultimate issue, and the Scriptures alone could offer reliable answers.

The lawyer not only knew where to look for the answer, but he also knew the right answer when he found it: "You shall love the Lord your God with all your heart, and with all your soul, and with all your strength, and with all your mind; and your neighbor as yourself" (Lk 10:27). Again Jesus' response was not antagonistic; it was supportive: "You have answered right; do this, and you will live." He joined the lawyer in *honoring the law of love*.

But Jesus did something more. He demanded that the law of love *be done*, linking a command to a promise. The lawyer did not miss the point. It made him edgy, uneasy, defensive. He knew that he was more proficient at debating the law than in doing it. So he took refuge behind his lawyer's armor, asking for a definition of terms: "And who is my neighbor?" There was no quarrel over the definition of God, but there *was* about the definition of a neighbor. What about Gentiles? Did Moses' command to love your neighbor (Lev 19:18) include them? Did it have tax collectors and sinners in mind? Did it extend to Roman soldiers? Or even Samaritans?

Jesus again refused to give a direct answer. Rather, he chose to let the lawyer discover his own answer, and to do so he told him what has probably become the most famous story in the world. But the disciples of Jesus, heady with newfound power, also had lessons to learn. The great commandments and obeying them daily were just as much a part of life in the kingdom as works of healing and announcements of judgment.

Jesus' rejoinder reminded them of life's true priorities: "Nevertheless do not rejoice in this, that the spirits are subject to you; but rejoice that your names are written in heaven" (Lk 10:20). Not power but relationship is what really counts. Not doing mighty works but being loved by God and responding wholeheartedly to his love is what we should value.

The disciples were enjoying high privilege—they were witnesses to the coming of God's kingdom. Jesus wanted them to remember this when he told them privately, "Blessed are the eyes which see what you see! For I tell you that many prophets and kings desired to see what you see, and did not see it, and to hear what you hear, and did not hear it" (10:23-24).

He also wanted them to remember the responsibilities of love that this privilege laid upon them. So Jesus told the lawyer a story of neighborly love, and he kept half an eye on his own men as he did so.

The Message: A Lesson in Love

My task is not to retell the story. Who dare try to improve on the brief but graphic version that Luke has preserved for us? When history's greatest storyteller is at work our lot is to listen and learn. We discover that the story is a lesson in love, picturing first *the importance of love*. Love is so important, so essential, that nothing substitutes for it.

Station yourself on that road from Jerusalem to Jericho. Watch that ruthless scene: the cruel robbery, the savage beating, the heartless abandonment—not even a garment left to shield the dying man from the stern heat of noontide or the harsh chill of midnight. Mark the men who come upon the lonely scene and inspect their credentials. The priest comes first, a descendant of Aaron's noble family and an heir of Levi's religious office. A man dedicated to the service of God, he was, like the lawyer, learned in the law. His record of faithfulness to the temple may have been outstanding. His knowledge of the prayers and hymns of Israel may have been exemplary.

And so with the Levite who passed by next. As part of the temple staff, he undoubtedly discharged his responsibilities with diligence—caring for the vessels, repairing the furnishings, participating in the music at the festive celebrations.

Both were honored and respected leaders. But none of this could substitute for love. At the moment when the scene cried for mercy, all other credentials were null and void. In fact, their official duties may have barred them from doing what the emergency required. It may not have been feelings of callousness but fear of contamination that moved them to the wrong side of the road. After all, men who handled the sacred vessels of the sanctuary were not to defile themselves by contact with a dead body. If the wounded traveler were to die on their hands they

would be excluded from service to God until after a
period of purification (Num 19:11-13).

Jesus' story also held before them *the possibility of
love*. From our vantage point beside the Jericho road,
we are surprised to see a Samaritan ride into view.
His garments and his accent clearly mark him as one
of the despised tribe living in what good Jews
branded a no man's land between Judea and Galilee.
His people had been mixed in blood and defiled in
worship since the days of the Assyrian captivity. His
forebears had conspired against Nehemiah's attempts to rebuild Jerusalem, and in his own lifetime
the Samaritan's countrymen had defiled the Jerusalem temple by strewing human bones in the court-
yard at Passover.

By introducing the Samaritan as the one who real-
izes the need for mercy and meets it, Jesus is declaring
that love is possible. Even an outcast can show it.
Love may come from surprising sources as God works
to meet human needs.

Finally, the details of the story call attention to *the
extent of love*. The pitiful state of the assaulted traveler, the possibility of harm to the Samaritan from
other robbers, the compassionate first aid, the journey to the inn, the payment of the bill, the promise of
further pay—all combine to picture the lengths to
which neighborly love must go.

The lawyer's query, "And who is my neighbor?"
suggested limits as to who is loved and what love
does. Jesus' story erased those limits.

The Demand: A Call for Mercy
The lawyer was trapped into giving the right answer
as to which of the three men proved neighbor to the

victim: "The one who showed mercy on him" was his grudging response. All of us who have heard the story with him say, "Yes, that is right!" to his answer.

But when we do, we too face the demand of the parable: "Go and do likewise" (Lk 10:37). With the lawyer, we are called not to debate the meaning of love, but to act on it. With the lawyer, we are ordered not to quibble over who our neighbor is, but to be a good neighbor wherever our acts and words of mercy can make a difference.

Mercy to the helpless is a kingly grace. Sons and daughters of the kingdom may well revel in their spiritual power. But they show themselves most like the Lord whose kingdom they proclaim when, in his name, they render deeds of mercy.

Prayer: Thank you, Father, that Jesus did more than define neighborliness for us. Thank you that he also demonstrated it. Let your royal love free us from apathy, selfishness and prejudice that we may bring healing to the robbed and wounded that cross our crowded ways. Through Jesus Christ who showed us how. Amen.

5

The Prodigal Son

A Royal Welcome

Luke 15:11-32

JESUS' CONFLICT WITH THE SCRIBES and Pharisees was not a superficial one. No bystander seeking to make peace in the midst of controversy could have said to the Pharisees, "I think you and Jesus are really saying the same thing in two different ways."

The conflict was deep, not just because the adversaries clung stubbornly to their points of view, but because the issue was of ultimate importance. Nothing less was at stake than the very nature of God. "What is God like?" was the question that lay at the heart of the debate. The scribes and Pharisees had one answer. Jesus had another.

The Setting: No Good News for Sinners
Luke's account shows how incensed the Jewish leaders were at Jesus' conduct: "Now the tax collectors and sinners were all drawing near to hear him. And the Pharisees and the scribes murmured, saying, 'This man receives sinners and eats with them'" (15:1-2).

It does not take much reading between the lines for us to see what they were really saying. "This man is not from God," their argument ran, "because God would not welcome sinners to his fellowship the way Jesus does." And if we followed their reasoning to the conclusion that seemed logical to them, it would end this way: "God is not like Jesus, eating with known scoundrels and lawbreakers; God is like us, careful in his contacts, scrupulous in his associations."

"There should be no good news for sinners" was the verdict of the scribes and Pharisees. To their minds, Jesus stepped completely out of God's will and ways by entering into conversation with sinners and even announcing to them, of all people, that God's kingdom was at hand. God would never do that, the Pharisees smugly concluded.

Their argument furnishes the setting for three great parables: the lost sheep, the lost coin and the lost sons. The plural *sons* is correct. It was not only the prodigal son who was lost; the son who remained home needed finding too.

Jesus voiced his disagreement with the religious leaders in story form, not in violent debate. By talking about sheep and shepherds, he got his questioners to agree that the lost were worth seeking and that finding them brought great joy. By speaking of coins, he brought them to admit that an all-out effort should be made to find even one that was lost and that a fruitful search set the neighborhood rejoicing. "God is like that," Jesus proclaimed. He not only welcomes sinners—including crooked, grasping tax collectors—he goes looking for them, like a shepherd. He not only receives unrighteous people, he values them as a peasant woman would treasure a lost coin. He searches out those who most need his help; and, when he finds them, he celebrates their recovery.

The kingdom of God was at hand. And it brought good news to all, even publicans and sinners—*especially* publicans and sinners.

The Message: A Father's Welcome to the Prodigal

With his deft touch, Jesus sketched the portraits of three characters with such clarity that we could almost recognize them if we met them on the street. With quick brush strokes and no wasted motion, the Master pictured the *younger son* asking for and then squandering his share of the family inheritance. The crowd that stood by, gazing at the portrait, would have understood well the customs to which Jesus alluded.

The younger son's share would have been one-third of the property, since by law (Deut 21:17) the elder son was heir to twice as much as any other son or, in this case, to the entire remainder of the father's estate (Lk 15:31). The young man's greed is seen in his selling off the property itself rather than merely living on its income. He wasted the capital as well as the interest of his inheritance. Accordingly, when he finally returned home, the only status legally open to him was that of a servant. He had both denounced and dissipated all his rights to sonship: "I will arise and go to my father, and I will say to him, 'Father, I have sinned against heaven and before you; I am no longer worthy to be called your son; treat me as one of your hired servants' " (15:18-19).

But the scribes and Pharisees would have done more than recognize the customs; they would have discerned the persons behind the portrait. As the sordid details developed—the overweening selfishness, the unbridled lust, the pagan degradation (the Jewish prodigal undoubtedly abandoned his religion by working on the sabbath and tending swine), the unrelieved squalor—the Pharisees would nod their heads in recognition. Who else could this decadent youth represent but the publicans and sinners who wasted their spiritual inheritance in the service of the world and the flesh?

Another figure began to take shape on the canvas —*the father*. No paint was spent on the father's response to his son's initial request. Jesus drew his viewers' attention to the scene of reconciliation in which the father threw dignity to the winds and raced to meet his son. The embrace of fellowship and the kiss of forgiveness were followed by the robe, the ring and the shoes.

The robe was a token of honor, an act of esteem usually reserved for special guests. The ring was a badge of authority, a signet whose stamp carried the right to buy and sell in the father's name. The shoes were a sign of wealth; they set the son apart from the peasants and the slaves of the land who walked barefoot down the roads of Palestine.

What an act of welcome, what a deed of redemption! In these few gestures the lad was lifted from shame to honor, from impotence to authority, from poverty to wealth. And all with merriment: "Bring the fatted calf and kill it, and let us eat and make merry; for this my son was dead, and is alive again; he was lost, and is found" (15:23-24).

The Pharisees were trapped. Jesus' story put a noose around their shoulders and drew them into the circle of his own thoughts about God. They needed no commentary to tell them who the father represented. Though they did not customarily refer to God as Father, they knew that Jesus did. Jesus was saying, "There *is* good news for sinners. There is the good news of a Father's welcome. There is the great joy of a lost son returned."

So far in the story Jesus had only made more detailed and more personal the point he had driven home when he spoke of a lost sheep and a lost coin. But when he turned to the third portrait, *the elder son,* he injected a new point, and with it sharply pricked the conscience of his audience. The sound of unplanned music, the report of an unheralded arrival and the news of an unscheduled feast grated on this son's sense of fairness. He protested to his father in measured spurts of anger: "Lo, these many years I have served you, and I never disobeyed your command; yet you never gave me a kid, that I might make merry with my friends. But when this son of yours came, who has devoured your living with harlots, you killed for him the fatted calf!" (15:29-30).

What scribe, what Pharisee could have missed the message? The portrait of that elder brother was a mirror in which they beheld their own selfishness.

His biting words were echoes of their own protests against Jesus' compassion for the outcasts of their society. They who prided themselves in knowing and following God's ways found themselves portrayed as the diametrical opposite of God. They had made God in their own image. And Jesus knew differently.

The Demand: Rejoicing at the Sight of Repentance
We are not told whether *they* could admit that he was right. But our loyalty to him demands that *we* admit that his picture of God is the only true one. His proclamation of God's compassion was backed by his demonstration of that same compassion, as evidenced by the way he himself acted toward publicans and sinners. Through Jesus the Christ, and through him alone, comes the full and true knowledge of God.

"What is God like?" remains life's most divisive question, yet the answer of the parable is the only lasting word of authority. We must hear Jesus Christ, God's only Son, saying, "God is like me." What a welcome word this is! We can hear it from the pigpens of our degradation, and we can follow its call all the way home. We can hear it from the Father's house and let it lead us out of our pride and self-righteousness. Wasteful younger children and spiteful elder children together can hear it and meet at the feast.

The Father's mood is joy wherever repentance is voiced. The repentance of squandered wealth and repentance of hoarded jealousy sound alike to him.

Prayer: Loving Father, waiting Father, welcoming Father, rejoicing Father, help us to see you as you are. Help us, from far country or near neighborhood, to return to your wide-open arms. Through Christ we pray. Amen.

The Rich Man and Lazarus

The Surprises of the Kingdom

Luke 16:19-31

JESUS' RUNNING QUARREL WITH the religious leaders was practical as well as theoretical. It centered on questions about keeping the sabbath, Jesus' claims to represent the Father and ways to obey the law. But it also dealt with matters like money.

As in many marriages, money became a touchy subject in Jesus' conversations with the Pharisees. The issue came to a head when the Savior attacked squarely the greed of his opponents: "No servant can serve two masters; for either he will hate the one and love the other, or he will be devoted to the one and despise the other. You cannot serve God and mammon" (Lk 16:13).

The Pharisees' response was predictable; they scoffed at Jesus. These "lovers of money" would have rationalized their interest in monetary matters. After all, did not more money mean more tithes to pay to the service of God? (The Pharisees put great stock in giving a tenth of everything to the Lord.) Furthermore, was not money, like all other material goods, a gift from God? Were they not to enjoy his blessings when he chose to send them?

Yet Jesus must have detected a hidden motive as his use of the word *mammon* suggests. This Aramaic word means simply money, but it can be used to indicate that money can get the best of us and mean too much to us. "Unrighteous mammon" is a phrase that Jesus used twice—almost in the sense of ill-gotten gain. And his phrase of *serving* mammon shows that the Pharisees were not just using their wealth; they were letting it rule them. It came close to being a god in their lives.

Material blessing was thought to be a sign of righteousness. To be wealthy, to be prosperous, was an indication that God was smiling favorably on their conduct. Surely, they argued, God would not pour out his beneficence on those with whom he was displeased. They viewed their comfortable homes, their lavish tables, their finely spun garments, their heavy purses as tangible evidence that God was on their side, pouring out his good will in response to their righteous deeds. They may have gone so far as to arch their eyebrows at Jesus' poverty. With no home of his own, no visible means of support, not even a purse, how could he lay claim to be God's righteous representative, the herald of a kingdom now at hand?

Jesus sensed their confusion and set out to put them straight: "You are those who justify yourselves before men," he proclaimed, "but God knows your hearts; for what is exalted among men is an abomination in the sight of God" (16:15).

Those words must have pinched a nerve. Jesus had branded them as idolators as the term *abomination* shows. They were not blessed by God in their wealth; they were counted abominable because that wealth had become their idol.

The Setting: Skepticism Demands a Sign

They were in for a surprise. The God who will tolerate no rival, not even the wealth which he has given, would in his time bring them low. They would be marked for judgment in company with everything else which he considers an abomination. They had not heard Mary's song, which sounded a theme of the new kingdom:

He has shown strength with his arm,
he has scattered the proud in the
    imagination of their hearts,
he has put down the mighty from
    their thrones,
and exalted those of low degree;
he has filled the hungry with good
    things,
and the rich he has sent empty away. (Lk 1:51-53)

They had not grasped the promises of Jesus, which contradicted their tightly held opinions:

Blessed are you poor, for yours is the kingdom of
    God.

> Blessed are you that hunger now, for you shall be
>   satisfied.
>
> Blessed are you that weep now, for you shall laugh.
>   (Lk 6:20-21)

They had not understood the woeful words of Jesus,
which announced the tragic reversal in the affairs of
the prosperous:

> But woe to you that are rich, for you have received
>   your consolation.
>
> Woe to you that are full now, for you shall hunger.
>
> Woe to you that laugh now, for you shall mourn
>   and weep. (6:24-25)

They would catch the meaning of Jesus' story, but
they would not like what they caught. In fact, the
story would catch *them*—and at two points where they
thought they were strong. The first, as we have seen,
was their conviction that their wealth was unques-
tionable evidence of God's blessing. The second point
was their confidence that their interpretation of God's
word was undebatable. The story of the rich man and
Lazarus must have staggered them with its truth.

The words of Jesus that Luke quoted just before
this story are puzzling: "The law and the prophets
were until John; since then the good news of the kingdom of God is preached, and every one enters it violently" (16:16). A new era was ushered in, Jesus
claimed, by the advent of John the Baptist and his
announcements that the kingdom was at hand. From
then on history would be divided into two epochs—
the old era in which God spoke through Moses and
the prophets, and the new era in which he sent John
and Jesus to herald the kingdom.

Furthermore, the transition from one epoch to the
other was wrenching. All who cast their lots with the

new kingdom violently rejected old ways, old relationships, old friends. Goods and kindred were let go if necessary, so valuable and so costly was the new life that Jesus offered.

Yet Moses and the prophets were still God's law and had to be hearkened to. But they were to be heard in terms of the kingdom; they were to be read not as ends in themselves but as part of the preparation for the kingdom. In that sense the law and the prophets were of eternal value: "But it is easier for heaven and earth to pass away, than for one dot of the law to become void" (v. 17). Jesus indirectly accused the Pharisees of a skepticism that did not truly trust God—a skepticism that relied on money, as a sign of God's blessing, a skepticism that did not really believe God's Word through Moses and the prophets.

The Message: Faith Obeys God's Word
According to Jesus, seeking signs of God's blessing is not what believing people should do. Take the life of the rich man who had every sign of blessing: splendid garments dyed with purple, fine linen robes and a sumptuous table (not just on occasion but every day). Any one who looked at him would have exclaimed, "Surely the hand of God is on him for good!"

Lazarus, however, was a beggar, not a wealthy man; full of sores, not ripe with health; at the gate, not at the table; hungry for scraps, not feasting lavishly. The likely verdict of the throngs that passed him was, "Surely the hand of God is on him for evil. What heinous sin did he or his parents commit that God would so punish him?" Jesus' hearers would have been full of admiration bordering on envy for the rich man, and full of pity edging toward scorn for the poor man. The second scene brought the surprise.

Death came to both men. The poor man was conveyed by angels to Abraham's bosom; the rich man found himself in Hades—tortured not merely by thirst, but by the sight of Lazarus's tranquil fellowship with the Abraham whose proud son the rich man had always claimed to be. The one man's pride and selfishness had been unmasked; the other man's humility and piety had been revealed. The man who served mammon was receiving the only reward mammon was prepared to pay; the man who served God was heir to the promises of God. Jesus had illustrated his own saying, "For what is exalted among men is an abomination in the sight of God."

The next scene brought a second surprise. The rich man had become the beggar, desperate for a drop of water. Abraham informed him that God's judgment was final. No water could be brought from one realm to the other. Realizing his hopeless plight, the rich man sought to warn his brothers, begging Abraham to send Lazarus as a courier of warning: "Send him to my father's house, for I have five brothers, so that he may warn them, lest they also come into this place of torment" (vv. 27-28). Then the surprise—Abraham answered, "If they do not hear Moses and the prophets, neither will they be convinced if some one should rise from the dead" (v. 31). Faith does not seek signs like the dramatic appearance of a man long dead.

Faith obeys God's Word about the dangers of selfishness and the importance of generosity. Faith obeys God's Word on the perils of idolatry and the foolishness of presuming on God's grace. Faith obeys God's Word as it promises a Redeemer, a Prophet, a King.

All this the Jewish leaders had failed to do. Their seeking of a sign that God blessed, that God approved, that God was at work, was skepticism. Jesus' story surprised them with its lesson of trust.

The Demand: Discipleship That Trusts the Lord

It surprises us as well, correcting our thinking about the way God works and speaks. True disciples do not look for signs. They trust God, come what may. If wealth and comfort are his gifts, they take no credit for earning them. If poverty and suffering are his will, they trust him to work his purposes in them. True disciples trust God to make his plan and his person known through his Word. They seek to be faithful to what God has said through Moses and the prophets, through Jesus and the apostles.

True disciples enjoy God's surprises. They are constantly surprised by the goodness of God amid the smart of pain and by the truth of God among the confusions of uncertainty. And they will be especially surprised by the love of God when death carries them, not merely to the bosom of Abraham, but to the Savior's gracious side.

Prayer: Lord, as we see examples of those who thought they knew your ways and missed them badly, lead us in the path of righteousness, for Christ's name's sake. Amen.

7

Building the Tower

The Cost of the Kingdom

Luke 14:25-33

MISUNDERSTANDING AND OPPOSITION were not the only problems Jesus faced. Popularity dug pitfalls for him as deep as did obscurity or hostility. The crowds pressed upon him, eager for his words, desperate for his touch.

We can understand why. For many of them, religious faith had become a matter of nostalgia. They remembered their past, the dramatic rescue that God had worked for their fathers in Egypt. But they had little sense of his dynamic intervention in their own lives.

Then came Jesus, in whom they felt the power of God's own words and deeds. Their hopes were stirred. Perhaps as Moses had brought release from Egypt so Jesus would wrest their freedom from Rome. They may have dreamed that the good old days would return and that a king would dwell in glory among them, as a son of David and Solomon.

It had been nearly a thousand years since a miracle worker had walked among the people with the might of an Elijah or Elisha. They knew the stories of lepers who were cleansed, of widows whose sons were revived from death, of pots of oil that kept on pouring— but they were stories of the past, not happenings of the present. Yet Jesus was a live reality before their very eyes. To him, as to an agent of God, they had brought their blind, their lame, their paralyzed, their deaf and dumb. And each time, Jesus' might had met their expectations.

Week by week in the synagogues the more devout of them heard the law's demands expounded with relentless rigor. Day by day in the streets the less devout felt the condemning glance of Pharisee and scribe who offered them no *shalom* of peace and welfare. Burdened by the law's requirements or frustrated by their lot as outcasts, they yearned for a word of aid and comfort. Then Jesus came, not with the meticulous arguments of a religious lawyer, but with the life-changing promises of a prophet of God. An office they thought dead, he had reactivated. A ministry long since past, he had reinstated.

The Setting: The Enthusiasm of the Throngs
What concerned Jesus, as the throngs enthusiastically dogged his every step, was not his personal safety

or the conservation of his energies, although he frequently pulled away to a quiet place for prayer and privacy. What concerned Jesus was the well-being of those who followed him. He knew that they would be deeply hurt if they miscalculated the cost of following him.

The enthusiasm of the throngs tempted him, for he loved people and felt compassion for their needs. He longed to free them from their bondage—whether religious, physical, emotional or spiritual. He was tempted to let them follow him; indeed to urge them to follow him. But the crowds were courting disaster because of their wide-eyed wonder.

First, *their relationships with their families were in jeopardy*. On one occasion, as Luke observed, "great multitudes accompanied him; and he turned and said to them, 'If any one comes to me and does not hate his own father and mother and wife and children and brothers and sisters, yes, and even his own life, he cannot be my disciple' " (14:25-26). This was strange talk from one whose rule was love, from one who lived to fulfill a law that called for the honoring of parents. Jesus purposely used strong language—"If any one comes to me and does not *hate* ... "—to sharpen the issues. Following him was not a free ticket to the bread and circuses of pleasure-filled living. There were demands so high that vital family links had to be deemed less important. Love and loyalty to the kingdom of God were to be so strong that natural affections were to seem like hate in comparison. To follow Jesus meant to subordinate all other loyalties to him.

Second, *Their loyalty to Jesus might cost them their lives*. He declared, "Whoever does not bear his own cross and come after me, cannot be my disciple" (v. 27). Letting go of family ties was keenly painful, especially for Jews who often lived in clans, who treasured family ties, who honored their father's name, whose sense of identity was derived from their kinships. But here Jesus was asking more. Bearing a cross was not the same as bearing a burden. Jesus' invitation was not to put up with inconvenience, or even to endure hardship, but to face death, a death like his on a cross.

The Message: The Requirements of the Master
Even the literary form of Jesus' message to the crowds helps to show how sober Jesus wanted us to be about our decision to follow him: he reinforced his point by telling two stories. Repetition was a Hebrew way of reasoning; therefore, a double story doubled or more than doubled the effect of the argument. The message centers in what Jesus expected of those who would go with him. Two requirements stand out in both stories.

Before you decide to follow Jesus, *take time to consider your decision.* "For which of you, desiring to build a tower, does not first sit down and count the cost, whether he has enough to complete it? . . . Or what king, going to encounter another king in war, will not sit down first and take counsel whether he is able with ten thousand to meet him who comes against him with twenty thousand?" (vv. 28, 31).

Some decisions in life can be made on the run. We do not brood long over what tie to snatch from the closet rack, what newspaper to buy at the local stand, what flavor to select at the ice-cream parlor. But where the cost is huge (as in building a tower) or the stakes are high (as in marching an army), we take time to consider. We sit down to do this, Jesus suggests. Following him in discipleship is much closer to the weighty decisions of a builder or a ruler than it is to our flip choices of tie, newspaper or ice cream.

What is involved in building a tower? A proper site must be chosen and an accurate plan drawn up. Material must be gathered and workers engaged. Length of time must be estimated and the effect of the weather predicted. Design, budget and timing must all be weighed—not along the way, not on the run, but by sitting down and taking time to consider them.

What is involved in sending an army to battle? Not only must the logistics of your troops be assessed, the possible strategies of any enemy must be analyzed: the strength and experience of their troops, their familiarity with the terrain, the length of their supply lines, the alternative routes open to them.

What is involved in following the Savior? Our allegiances are altered sharply—we now belong to a King whose demands come first. Our hopes are reordered drastically—we jettison our old props and lean only on Jesus Christ. Our values are turned around—giving, not getting; reaching out to others, not protecting ourselves from others. What we once held dear—our goods, our money—we now deem expendable. What we once disdained—humble service to those around us—now becomes our highest joy. Persons that we envied for their power and wealth we now pity because of their moral ignorance, their spiritual insensitivity.

Before you decide to follow Jesus, *look to the consequences of your decision.* An unfinished tower is a source of shame: "Otherwise, when he has laid a foundation, and is not able to finish, all who see it begin to mock him, saying, 'This man began to build, and was not able to finish' " (vv. 29-30). If an unfinished construction project brings shame, how much more does halfhearted discipleship? Imagine breaking your family ties, losing your job, changing your whole way of life as those early disciples often did, and then not following through. It would be better not to start than to turn back.

An ill-fought battle carries the threat of disaster. If one king is not sure of victory over the other, "while the other is yet a great way off, he sends an embassy and asks terms of peace" (v. 32).

If an ill-conceived military campaign brings disaster, how much more does turncoat discipleship? The person who turns back suffers the guilt, the shame and the disappointment of defeat. Discouragement spreads among the faithful and doubt among those who do not yet believe.

Look to the consequences, Jesus pleads. Total commitment, not temporary enthusiasm, is what the kingdom costs.

The Demand: The Renunciation of All
Come to me, come with me, reads the invitation of Jesus. But only the serious need respond. Nothing less than the renunciation of what we have and are will do. Our Lord summarized his demands in bluntest prose: "So therefore, whoever of you does not renounce all that he has cannot be my disciple" (v. 33).

The Lord is not saying that the way to the kingdom is paved with negatives. But he is saying that the decision to follow Jesus is such a colossal yes to his will and ways that it means a decisive no to everything else.

Prayer: Heavenly Father, hammer our soft enthusiasm into hard resolve. Teach us to count the cost of our discipleship and then to see that it is worth any cost we are called to pay. In our Savior's compelling name we pray. Amen.

8

Laborers in the Vineyard

The Grace of the King

Matthew 19:23–20:16

THEIR EYES WERE MOIST AS they watched the young man trudge sorrowfully away. He had come to the brink of commitment and then turned aside. At the Master's urging he had sat down to count the cost of the kingdom and had found that cost too high. The promise of heavenly treasure did not loom large enough to lure him from his earthly treasure. Matthew's description is both succinct and sad: "When the young man heard this [Jesus' call to sell his goods and give the proceeds to the poor] he went away sorrowful; for he had great possessions" (19:22).

Jesus watched quietly as the man disappeared in the distance then, in those familiar words, sighed in regret, "Truly, I say to you, it will be hard for a rich man to enter the kingdom of heaven." The astonished disciples wondered if *anyone* could be saved, but Jesus reminded them of the One to whom belonged the task of salvation: "With men this is impossible, but with God all things are possible."

Peter's thoughts had not wandered from the rich young man, by then just a speck on the horizon. By holding on to his wealth he had lost the reward of heaven, or at least was in danger of losing it. The contrast between that young man and Jesus' followers struck Peter sharply and he said, "Lo, we have left everything and followed you. What then shall we have?"

The Setting: A Question about Rewards

Peter's question sparked the story of the vineyard owner and his strange policy of paying wages. But first Jesus answered Peter directly:

> Truly, I say to you, in the new world, when the Son of man shall sit on his glorious throne, you who have followed me will also sit on twelve thrones, judging the twelve tribes of Israel. And every one who has left houses or brothers or sisters or father or mother or children or lands, for my name's sake, will receive a hundredfold, and inherit eternal life. But many that are first will be last, and the last first. (vv. 28-30)

"Rewards there will be," was Jesus' answer. "What will you have, Peter? You will share my authority in the world to come. You apostles will be part of my administrative staff, governing the tribes of Israel. And any one else who has met the cost of the kingdom by letting goods and kindred go will receive bountiful rewards. Do not be surprised that God works differently from human beings. People who seem to be tops here in power, wealth and prestige may be placed at the bottom there. And those whose names have not been prominent, whose reputations have not been celebrated, whose wealth has not been notable may be counted first as the God of grace gives out his rewards."

Jesus went on to tell the story about the householder and his wage scale. The story was about God. The spotlight was not on the workers, as faithful and diligent as they had been. The gracious landowner held center stage.

The Message: A Lesson in Grace
With all the talk about rewards in Peter's question and Jesus' answer, it would have been easy for the disciples to think about rewards as payment for merit. The harder and longer we work, the greater our responsibilities, the more we are paid. The Jewish leaders who helped shape the thinking of their people certainly believed this. Rewards for them were a system of works, a closely kept record of performance and achievement. God was the careful accountant who meted out payment and punishment, measure for measure.

"Not so," Jesus countered. "If you read God as a legalistic human manager, a stickler for accuracy, a penny-pinching employer who only pays what he must and begrudges that, you have misread him entirely. Let me tell you what God is really like." He told the story in two parts. The first described the landowner's program of paying laborers; the second recounted the complaints of the laborers who had worked longer than others and yet received the same pay.

The two halves of the parable are parts of a twofold lesson in grace, the first of which is *a demonstration of grace.* The householder entered into a wage agreement with a crew of laborers. It was the height of the harvest, so haste was essential if the grapes were to be picked and pressed before the rainy season set in. The workers were sent out early (perhaps about 6:00 A.M.) to get a head start on the day's work. They agreed to the denarius as satisfactory pay, for it was the standard wage. There is no hint that the owner drove a sharp bargain with them. He was utterly just in the compensation he offered, and they eagerly accepted his terms.

But the crop was abundant and the time short, so the owner returned to the marketplace where workers waited to be hired. By now it was the third hour (that is, about 9:00 A.M.), and the second crew of workers joined the first. They were promised the appropriate pay for their work: "You go into the vineyard too, and whatever is right I will give you" (20:4). Undoubtedly they expected about three-quarters of a denarius for their work. (The denarius was not the smallest Roman coin, so the owner could readily pay each worker the proper fraction for his labor.)

The owner made two more trips to the marketplace —one about noon, the other at three o'clock. We can assume in each instance that the workers were promised "whatever was right" for their hours of labor. Not content with the pace and volume of the work, the owner made a last-minute trip to the marketplace at about 5:00 P.M. There he found a group of workers who had dawdled in the market all day, hired by no one. The householder's sense of urgency combined with his feelings of compassion, and he sent them into the vineyard as the sun dipped low over the western hills.

The sun set and all work ceased. The workers gathered round the steward to receive their pay. Only those who had worked all day knew the terms of their contract. Impatiently they waited for their wages, anticipating the gleaming denarius in their sweaty palms as the foreman paid them. But the foreman did a strange thing. He called to be paid first those who had been hired last. And to their surprise—and everyone else's—he gave them a shiny denarius, a full day's pay for an hour's work.

The owner demonstrated his grace by giving as many workers as possible an opportunity to earn some money. Food for their tables was surely one of his concerns, for he hired even the less skilled and the less industrious. In a labor pool like that Palestinian marketplace, the reputation of each person would be known to the various employers and they would naturally choose the strongest workers first. But the owner in the story saw to it that every one was put to work. He also demonstrated his grace in the wages he paid. No one was cheated. The owner kept his word all the way. But he saw to it that all got a day's pay, no matter how late they had been hired.

The workers who had toiled for twelve hours or more grumbled, "These last worked only one hour, and you have made them equal to us who have borne the burden of the day and the scorching heat" (20:12).

In their fatigue they mistook grace for injustice, begrudging the owner's generosity because they thought it unfair to them. "Friend, I am doing you no wrong," the vineyard owner replied to one of them. "Did you not agree with me for a denarius? Take what belongs to you, and go; I choose to give to this last as I give to you. Am I not allowed to do what I choose with what belongs to me?" (vv. 13-14).

Here was a lesson in the *appreciation of grace*. Grace never does less than justice demands, but it has the freedom to do much more. The owner had the right to be as gracious as he chose, providing he kept his word and dealt fairly with his laborers. When he did, each was to accept gratefully what his grace provided and not to look grudgingly on the wages of anyone else.

God the King gives and will give abundant rewards. But they will be reflections of his grace more than recognition of our merit. In addition, they will be given on God's terms. Like the owner of the busy vineyard, God may call workers of varying skills at different times in the day. When the final reckoning comes at history's close, he will demonstrate his freedom to decide who is paid and how much.

The Demand: A Call to Humility

The parable put two groups of hearers on the spot, demanding a change of mind and a new outlook. It brought fresh truth about God himself, picturing him as the kind, compassionate God who pities hungry workers and pays them beyond their due. This fresh truth insisted on a fresh response: it called all its hearers to humility.

It called *Jewish leaders* to look again at the good news of the kingdom. Jesus' words and actions troub-

led them primarily because they had a wrong understanding of God's nature. They refused to believe
that the riffraff of their society could participate in
the kingdom. They insisted that the invitations being
sent to harlots, lawbreakers and tax collectors carried
the wrong addresses. God is just and would not reward such blatant sinners with his blessing.

Jesus called these religious experts to humility:
"Look at what God is really like and your attitude
toward his grace will change. You will be grateful for
whatever comes your way and not grumble over what
happens to others."

The parable also called *Jesus' disciples* to humility.
They who had followed from the beginning were in
for a rich reward, including the shared authority of
Christ, the hundredfold compensation and the de-
light of eternal life. Others would come later, suffer
less, bear lighter burdens, carry milder pressure. Yet
the God of grace might choose to reward all alike.

Their job was not unlike ours. We too must make
the grand commitment that the rich young man was
loath to make. We too must labor for as many hours
as the Lord requires. We too must gladly accept whatever reward he gives. Jesus' story helps us do that.
By holding before us a picture of God's grace, it
readies our hearts to respond in trust. We work hard
—and on his terms. We do so gladly, confident that
his terms are terms of grace.

Prayer: Our Father, we do not ask that you will put
us last so that later we may be first. We only ask that
you will show us your own gracious face so that
whether we are first or last we may trust you fully and
find you fully true. Through Jesus who is the Savior.
Amen.

9

The Publican
and the Pharisee

The Road to Royalty

Luke 18:9-14

JESUS OFTEN USED SHARP contrasts to put across his point. He did this because he was a good teacher. He knew that we remember best what we can visualize as we hear it. So he spoke of good trees that bear good fruit and bad trees that bear bad fruit, making vivid the vast difference between those who serve God and those who do not.

He also used this device because he was a Jewish wise man, born to a Jewish mother, raised in a Jewish family, stamped by a Jewish culture. Setting up contrasts was a standard Jewish method of instructing or reasoning. Usually a promise of reward for good conduct was placed beside the threat of harm found in bad conduct. The first psalm is an example, where the wise man described the righteous person as a tree that prospers with fruit and the unrighteous person as a pile of chaff subject to the whim of the wind. Similarly, Jesus taught about the rocklike stability of the life built on obedience to his words and the sandlike shakiness of the life lived without heed to those words.

But these sharp contrasts do more than mark Jesus as an effective teacher whose techniques were drawn from his Hebrew background. He was also a sound theologian, and his sharp contrasts show how he distinguished the ways of God from the ways of men. To see the difference between the holy and loving God and the sinful, prideful human creature is to learn life's basic lesson. The command against the worship of other gods stands at the head of the Ten Commandments—and for good reason. To go wrong there throws us into complete confusion. Dial the wrong area code and no matter how accurate the other numbers may be the phone call goes awry. Miss the uniqueness of God, and all human purposes will be out of kilter.

The Setting: A False Understanding of Righteousness
We are not left in doubt about the purpose of the story of the Pharisee and the publican who went to the temple to pray. Luke says, "He also told this parable to some who trusted in themselves that they were righteous and despised others" (18:9). These Jewish leaders assumed that righteousness was something

they *did,* something within their power to *achieve.*
This was a massive error made by disregarding much
of what the Old Testament teaches about righteousness.

Righteousness in biblical terms is first and fore-
most *right relationship.* It means the recognition that
our lives depend wholly on God for what they have
and are. *Loyalty,* in the strongest sense, is as good a
synonym for it as any. The righteous are not those
who smugly perform their religious duties; they are
those who strongly cling to the God of grace. The
righteous are not those who have mastered the rituals
and regulations; they are those who cast themselves
on the love of God (while not understanding how
God could love them at all). The righteous go with
God because they know they have no other way to go,
not because they think they deserve to. Forgiveness
is what they need. Where else will they find it? Truth
is what they deem important. Is there any other
source of it? Purpose is what they desire. Who else
can flood their lives with it?

It is not surprising that those who "trusted in themselves that they were righteous" were also wrong in
their attitudes toward their fellow human beings.
Nothing can teach humility better than a bright vision
of who God is and how much we need him. Nothing
will spawn pride faster than a conviction that by our
own right deeds we have pleased the heavenly Father.
Such pride puts insuperable obstacles in the way of
sound human relationships, which are an aspect of
true righteousness. Luke's word about these proud
religious leaders was carefully chosen: they *despised*
others.

Pride puffs us up in our own minds so that others

look thin and shabby by comparison. It cuts us off from any contribution we can make to them or they to us by implying that we do not need each other. What self-satisfied person needs the fellowship of a doubting, failing struggler? What person afflicted by poverty of spirit would seek help from someone who views him or her with disdain?

The Message: A Passionate Plea for Mercy
The marked contrast between the Pharisee and the publican put the matter in the plainest possible light. The two types of men became stereotypes in Jesus' hand, characters as readily recognized by the Lord's hearers as cartoons of political celebrities are today.

Though the Pharisees numbered only a few thousand, they were highly influential and highly respected by the common people for whom they tried to make the law bearable. They might have made safe neighbors with their scrupulous honesty and their staunch commitment to the commands of God. One can hardly fault the Pharisee for shunning extortion, adultery and injustice as he noted in his prayer. Nor should he be blamed for fasting and tithing. His conduct was exemplary, right down to his realization of the importance of prayer, even thankful prayer.

The publican, on the other hand, was a model of all that the Jews, leaders and commoners alike, resented. The word *despised* would be among the gentler labels that he bore. First, he was an agent of Rome in a time when Palestine was an occupied territory virtually under military rule. Citizens were forced to pay taxes to a regime they loathed and to a nation whose way of life was an abomination. To make matters worse, the taxes were both exorbitant and unjust, literally a form of the extortion from which the Pharisee was thankful to be free. And to pour salt in the Jewish wounds, the Roman tax contractors used their wealth not for stable government or civic improvements but to feather their own nests.

The contrast, then, was one of the Master's sharpest: a distinguished teacher of the law and a degraded ally of the enemy. Both were praying. Their prayers were appropriately different—or so it seemed. Confidently the Pharisee reminded God of his own good works. Contritely the publican beat his breast and begged for mercy. But Jesus did not leave the interpretation of the story to the intuition of his audience. Bluntly he announced, "I tell you, this man went down to his house justified rather than the other" (18:14).

What does it take to be right with God? Repentance is the plain answer. Where is the key to righteousness found? In pleading for mercy is Jesus' response. Which path merges with the road to royalty? The path of humiliation is the correct reply.

The Demand: A Strong Incentive to Humility

God's ways are not man's ways. In our frailty we admire strength in others and covet it for ourselves. We salute the successful physician, the influential lawyer, the skilled preacher, the accomplished chef, the disciplined athlete. We are tempted to brand these traits "Godlike."

But God knows better. None of us can compete with him; none of us can add to his stature; none of us can pass his standards. Even to try is wrong. The demand that the parable puts upon all of us is *humility:* "For every one who exalts himself will be humbled, but he who humbles himself will be exalted" (v. 14). The only way to please God is to give up trying and to cast ourselves on his love. It is God's credential of grace that counts, not our credential of achievement. If that publican could be justified—counted right with God, accepted as his child, cleared of sin—so can all of us.

We must waste no time thanking God that we are not like the treacherous, money-grabbing publicans —nor like the self-righteous Pharisee. Rather we must thank God that his mercy covers our sins, his power strengthens our weakness, his light brightens our darkness, his path is the road from wretchedness to royalty.

Prayer: Holy Father, this story leaves us with no alternatives. We gladly abandon ourselves to your mercy, confident that what your grace provides is beyond not only what we deserve but beyond what we can ask or think. Through Jesus Christ, the sinner's friend, we pray. Amen.

10

The Wicked
Vinedressers

The Anger of the King

Matthew 21:33-43

JESUS' DAYS ON EARTH HAD dwindled to a handful. He had entered his final, fatal week, which captured the essence of much of his ministry. The common people greeted him with enthusiasm; the religious leaders eyed him with resentment. Both responses reached a climax during the busy days of what we have come to call Holy Week.

The acclaim of the crowds reached fever pitch on the Sunday when they gave Jesus a royal welcome of garments and branches spread along his pathway amid shouts of "Hosanna to the Son of David! Blessed is he who comes in the name of the Lord! Hosanna in the highest!" His reputation had so preceded him that the throngs had no trouble identifying him as "the prophet Jesus from Nazareth of Galilee" (Mt 21:11).

If the praise of the multitudes reached its apex that day so did the resentment of their leaders. The conflict which had begun three years before with the first announcements that the kingdom of heaven was at hand was now to sharpen into bitter battle and to culminate in a plot of death.

None of this caught Jesus by surprise. He had spoken freely with his disciples about his death. Now he revealed its inevitability in a story which summarized the spiritual history of the Jewish religious hierarchy. He told of an absentee landowner who prepared a vineyard to bear profitable fruit. The man then turned over the operation of the vineyard to a group of tenants who had contracted to share a percentage of its produce with the owner. The plot of the parable centered in the owner's attempts to collect his share of the vineyard's fruit. He sent two groups of servants whom the tenants savagely beat, stoned and even killed. Finally, he sent his son in full hope that his authority would be respected. But even the son was rejected by the tenants and cruelly murdered.

The Setting: Final Rejection

Given the context in which this story is set, the description of Jesus' death does not seem strange. Episode after episode of his dealings with the religious bureaucrats betrays their mounting animosity toward him. On Palm Sunday he had entered the temple of

God in Jerusalem and upset all the merchants and moneychangers who were profiting from the religious devotion of the pilgrims from other lands. Not only had sheep, goats and pigeons been sold at outrageous prices, but also the rate of exchange for foreign coins amounted to robbery. Jesus declared, "It is written, 'My house shall be called a house of prayer'; but you make it a den of robbers" (v. 13).

The priests were outraged at his action. What right did he have to do violence to their precincts? What gave him a mandate to criticize the time-honored practices that prevailed in their temple courts? Their anger was compounded when the blind and the lame came to him for healing in those same courts, and especially when the shrill voices of little children also cried, "Hosanna to the Son of David!" The chief priests and scribes were indignant over his acclaim. The children were naming Jesus as the Messiah, an act of blasphemy in the eyes of the priests.

Later in the week they again confronted Jesus in the temple where he had come to teach. This time they were suspicious of his credentials and asked angrily, "By what authority are you doing these things, and who gave you this authority?" It was a form of bureaucratic red tape calculated to keep the real issues at arm's length. Perhaps they felt the little children were right in recognizing Jesus as Messiah and these feelings made them double their efforts to disgrace him. Almost nothing drives us more to prove that we are right than the growing suspicion that we are wrong.

Their challenge of Jesus' authority gave him further opportunity to prove how compelling his authority was. He put a question to them that was double-edged. They knew that on whatever side they grabbed it they would be cut, so they left it untouched. They refused to answer whether John's baptism was carried out by divine or only human authority. And, in turn, Jesus refused to say anything more about his own authority, showing just how much authority he had.

The drama of Christ's proclamation of the heavenly kingdom now present on earth was pushing toward its final act. Now the spotlight was not on the skeptical religious leaders nor the believing throngs; it was on the Master.

The Message: Certain Judgment

In a few brief lines Jesus put the issue squarely to his opponents: "Your quarrel is not with me, but with God; your rejection of his demands is not new, but old; your fate is not further blessing, but certain judgment." By using a parable to make his point, Jesus forced his hearers to render their own verdict of self-condemnation. They were trapped by his inexorable logic.

In the householder's preparation of the vineyard the audience would have recognized God's provision. They were thoroughly at home with the picture of Israel as the vineyard and God as the farmer. In Jesus' words the Jews would have heard reminders of Isaiah's famous song:

Let me sing for my beloved
    a love song concerning his vineyard:
My beloved had a vineyard
    on a very fertile hill.
He digged it and cleared it of stones,
    and planted it with choice vines;

he built a watchtower in the midst of it,
    and hewed out a wine vat in it;
and he looked for it to yield grapes,
    but it yielded wild grapes. (5:1-2)

Jesus said that God was still waiting for his share of the fruit. He had done all that a vineyard owner could be expected to do: he had carefully cleared the land of stones and then with the stones built a hedge on the borders and a watchtower in the center of the vineyard; he had tenderly planted each cutting in the ground and soaked its place with water; he had skillfully dug the winepress in two levels, the higher one for pressing, the lower one for collecting the juice, and a channel between them through which the pressed-out juice would drain.

The audience would also have recognized God's rights as the story progressed. Absentee landowners were not strange to them, nor were the contracts that such owners made with tenant farmers who worked the land and kept a share of the fruit (we would call this arrangement sharecropping). Land was rarely sold in old Palestine because it was viewed as an essential part of every family's heritage, retained by a family from generation to generation even when they no longer lived near the land.

As owner and planter of Israel God had rights to the fruit of his labors. Through Isaiah he has told us exactly what fruit he expected:

For the vineyard of the Lord of hosts
    is the house of Israel,
and the men of Judah
    are his pleasant planting;
and he looked for justice,
    but behold, bloodshed;

for righteousness,
   but behold, a cry! (5:7)
Justice and righteousness—concern for the needs of
others and full loyalty to God—were the fruits God
expected from his vineyard. What he got in Isaiah's
day were brutal bloodshed and the impassioned cry
of the oppressed.

In Jesus' time the fruit was scarcely more prom-
ising: empty ritual, hollow legalism, boastful arro-
gance. The rights of the vineyard owner were being
dolefully transgressed. Worse still, all his efforts to
exercise his rights were rigidly resisted. Like servants
sent to collect a percentage of the fruit, wave after
wave of prophets had come to remind the Israelites of
their obligations. Sometimes they were greeted with
stony silence; at other times with silent stones. Amos,
Isaiah, Jeremiah and others, some whose names we
do not know, had been opposed and persecuted by
the rich and the powerful. Finally, the Father had sent
the Son.

The audience listened to the story, increasingly
incensed by the actions of the tenants. When Jesus
asked them about the tenants' fate, they were burst-
ing with the answer: "He will put those wretches to a
miserable death, and let out the vineyard to other
tenants who will give him the fruits in their seasons"
(Mt 21:41). The Jewish leaders had brought in a verdict against themselves. Before they realized it they
had recognized God's wrath rightfully directed
against them in all its awesome holiness. They knew
that their judgment was certain.

The Demand: Fruitful Service
Listening to this story, we stand at one of history's

turning points. Jesus was signaling a transition in God's dealings with the human family. No longer were the sons and daughters of Abraham to be his major partners. God was making a crucial change in his program of revelation and redemption. Jesus did not mince words: "Therefore I tell you, the kingdom of God will be taken away from you and given to a nation producing the fruits of it" (v. 43).

The church, composed of Jew and Gentile, is the people of God, the holy nation called to bear his fruit. What a demand the parable places on us. We are the present sharecroppers, tenants of a land that God owns, raising crops to share with him. His standards have not changed nor his demands diminished. Fruit is his due; fruit he will have—either from us or from others. Familiar as we are with the anger of the King, we pledge ourselves to be fruitful subjects sharing his passion for love and justice. God is not through with Israel; in due season they will again participate in his glorious service. But in this lengthy "meanwhile," the opportunity is ours. We must not miss it.

Prayer: Holy Father, we are unworthy, unprofitable servants at our best unless your grace stirs us to generosity and compassion. Let this stern story be a messenger of grace urging us to live for you. Through your gracious Son we pray. Amen.

The Wise and Foolish Maidens

The Royal Wedding

Matthew 25:1-13

THE SCENE WAS FAMILIAR to Jesus' audience. The married folks (virtually all the adults) looked at each other fondly, their eyes moist with nostalgia as they remembered their wedding nights. The young men nudged each other knowingly, their eyes gleaming with anticipation as each one imagined that it was his own wedding which Jesus was describing. The young women blushed and coyly turned their heads from the gaze of the young men.

Jesus pictured a wedding procession which began

when friends of the bride-to-be arrived at her house and, with her, waited for the bridegroom. Custom in Palestine had it that the bridegroom would visit the bride's home and walk with her and her friends in a torchlight procession to his home where the actual marriage ceremony took place. In this parable the focus is not so much on the final feast or the wedding service as on the steps that lead up to it. Everyone who heard Jesus that day had watched or participated in the "waiting game" and procession, though the details of the procedure differed from region to region and even village to village.

Jesus' hearers could picture the excited maidens dressing themselves in their best garments, picking up the torches they needed to light the way in the dark, and then scurrying and chattering all the way to the house of the bride. There were ten of them in the story, divided into two groups of five. All ten were dressed alike; all ten shared the excitement of the event; all ten carried torches. But only five thought to bring flasks of oil in which to soak their torches when the time for the procession came.

Jesus called the two groups "wise" and "foolish" because one was prepared for the needs of the night; the other was not. We are not told why the bridegroom in the parable was delayed. Perhaps he was enjoying his last moments of singleness with his bachelor friends. Whatever the reason, he was so long in coming to his bride's home that her ten friends, fatigued from the excitement of the evening, dropped off to sleep. They were awakened by a cry from outside the house, "Behold, the bridegroom! Come out to meet him" (Mt 25:6). Quickly they rose and grabbed their torches. It was at that moment that the foolish maidens discovered their mistake.

As they watched their wise friends pour oil on the rags that were wrapped around a stick to form a torch, they realized they had forgotten their flasks. The hour was midnight; the sky was black; no lamps flickered in the homes along the way. Without a torch the journey was not safe; without a torch they could not share the festive mood of the procession. Dejected and frustrated they hurried to a shop near the marketplace to bang on the shopkeeper's door, rouse him from his sleep and bargain for some oil. Remorsefully they watched the procession wend its way through the dawn. Regretfully they heard the sounds of laughter, the shouts of glee as the wedding party threaded its way through the narrow streets to the bridegroom's home. Occasionally they caught glimpses of the wise maidens' gleaming torches.

By the time the sleepy oil vendor had been roused from his bed and persuaded by the pleading maidens to sell them some oil, the torches had disappeared in the distance and the laughter was beyond their hearing. In a panic they soaked their torches, splashing olive oil on themselves in the process. Like frightened birds they ran to catch up, but they could not. Out of breath, they arrived at the wedding house only to find the doors firmly barred. From within, the sounds of festivity bubbled forth, but their knocking and pounding were in vain. A wedding was an intimate affair not open to intruders, whether their motive was to join the merriment or to disrupt it. The householder's response to the five maidens was exactly what it would have been to anyone else who had sought entrance: "Truly, I say to you, I do not know you" (v. 12).

The Setting: A Lack of Careful Preparation
The men and women to whom Jesus came were not
prepared either. As John commented in his Gospel,
"He was in the world, and the world was made
through him, yet the world knew him not. He came to
his own home, and his own people received him not"
(1:10-11). Jesus' story, therefore, looked both forward
and backward. It was both a reminder that the Jews
had been unprepared for his first coming and a warning that everyone should be prepared for his second
coming.

Most Jews were unprepared because they looked
for the wrong signs. They waited for pomp and splen-
dor, for burning judgment and fiery majesty, for a
noble kingdom and a glorious throne. They missed
the wedding; they were not ready for the Bridegroom.
Their lack of preparedness marked them for judgment: "The men of Nineveh will arise at the judgment
with this generation and condemn it; for they re-
pented at the preaching of Jonah, and behold, something greater than Jonah is here. The queen of the
South will arise at the judgment with this generation
and condemn it; for she came from the ends of the
earth to hear the wisdom of Solomon, and behold,
something greater than Solomon is here" (Mt 12:
41-42).

The Message: A Need for Joyful Vigilance
"Be ready for the wedding," said Jesus to his people.
"Be joyfully vigilant," though there is much to en-
dure that would threaten our joy while we wait for
Christ's return.

Be joyful despite the appearance of false messiahs:
"Take heed that no one leads you astray. For many

will come in my name, saying, 'I am the Christ,' and they will lead many astray" (Mt 24:4-5). We can follow the wrong messiah and be seduced into thinking that the Bridegroom has come and that we are on the way to the wedding. How many people today have gotten trapped into false cults that claim to be the fulfillment of Jesus' promises without the truth, the power and the glory which his kingdom will reveal?

We can also miss the wedding by assuming that there will be no wedding. One of the by-products of the false Christs is the disillusionment and disappointment which people suffer. "All religion is a hoax," they are apt to conclude. "All that talk of Christ's coming for history's most glorious wedding is hokum. I won't believe in any of it, not even what the Christian church has taught for all these centuries."

Be joyful despite the occurrence of calamities: "And you will hear of wars and rumors of wars; see that you are not alarmed; for this must take place, but the end is not yet. For nation will rise against nation, and kingdom against kingdom, and there will be famines and earthquakes in various places: all this is but the beginning of the birth-pangs" (Mt 24:6-8). We can miss the wedding by misreading the events of history. If we presume that everything will get better and better and that Christ will come to polish off this gradual process of improvement, we will miss the meaning of his coming. Things indeed may get much worse before he comes.

We do not relish war. We do not rejoice in famine. We do not applaud earthquakes. But when these calamities hit, we can remember Jesus' warnings and look beyond them. Others may be craven with fear of these disasters (we had two earthquakes in Pasadena this morning), but we can hear in and through the conflicts of nations and the catastrophes of nature the cheering words of Jesus, "Be ready for the wedding."

Be joyful despite the onslaught of tribulation: "Then they will deliver you up to tribulation, and put you to death; and you will be hated by all nations for my name's sake" (Mt 24:9). Waiting for the wedding will be painful because neither the Groom nor the bride will be universally loved. Tribulation will be part of normal Christian experience, especially just before the end.

The Demand: A Call for Strong Evaluation

Are we ready or are we not? It is not self-examination that Jesus demands but strong examination, which his Word and his Spirit can best perform. Ours is the task of opening our lives to their scrutiny. Theirs is the task of telling us how we measure up.

Are we ready and waiting joyfully for the wedding? Despite the false messiahs, despite the disasters of war and famine, despite the pending tribulation, our waiting is to be steeped in joy. It is *the* wedding—the permanent union of Jesus and his people, the full fellowship of God with his own children, the endless beginning of a new life and a new world.

Prayer: Our Father, keep our minds single, our faith strong, our hopes secure. Let the torches of our waiting be soaked with the oil of your Spirit till the Bridegroom comes. In his name we pray. Amen.

Conclusion

Our daughter, Mary, warned me years ago of the dangers of this kind of book. As a teen-ager she showed irritation, justifiably I suppose, when I imposed on her my amateurish talent as a drama critic. After a movie or play, I would raise the issue, "What do you suppose the writer was trying to say?" Usually she would duck the question or flip it back to me with, "What do *you* think?" One night, when her patience wore thin, her answer to my question exploded: "Oh, Dad! Why do you have to analyze everything? Why can't you just sit there and enjoy the movie?"

Those who have persevered through my analysis of a dozen or more parables may sympathize with Mary's reaction. Why not let the stories speak for themselves as they did in Jesus' day? By now my response may be predictable: we do not live in Jesus' time or place. One aim of my interpretation has been to transplant us to that ancient context, and place us beside those to whom the parables were first uttered. And even they needed help to understand them, as Mark's note informs us: "but privately to his own disciples he explained everything" (4:34).

The subject was too important to leave its interpretation to chance. It still is. At stake is our understanding of God's kingdom and our commitment to it. To proclaim that kingdom we must be ready to "leave the dead to bury their own dead" (Lk 9:60). To participate in that kingdom we must be willing to keep hand to plow and not look back to those at home (Lk 9:62). Therefore, any light cast on the character and call of that kingdom is welcome. Jesus taught his parables to interpret it, as he worked his miracles to demonstrate it. It is the theme of his ministry, the purpose of his death, the message of his resurrection and the aim of his second coming. If the importance of God's rule in history has been highlighted and the purposes and power of that rule have been illuminated, then my goal has almost been achieved.

But not quite. The goal of the parables is also to warm our hearts with dedication. The kingdom is not only a mystery to be explained; it is a mandate to be obeyed. It is God at work in Jesus, calling each of us to repentance, faith, service and hope. It is a new kingdom; to share in it, each of us must be made new.

To point out the need for that newness was the ultimate purpose of these chapters. But they themselves are not the means of it. No human words ever can be. For that we must look again and again to the parables of the new kingdom. And to him who spoke in such magnificent pictures.